Contents

Managing Difficult Behaviour

We've all had times when our usual way of managing difficult behaviour isn't working. Times of broken sleep, toddler tantrums, food fussiness, fighting, not talking or worrying about friends.

In *Managing Difficult Behaviour* we will help you think about how you interact with your children, show you how to adapt to different personalities and work towards greater cooperation.

Our key basics are:

- A warm and loving relationship with the child.
- Avoiding battles, not winning them, is a sign of maturity.
- Reward is more effective than punishment.
- Biggest is not best when it comes to rewards and punishments.
- Your positive attention is what your child wants most.

We use 'he' and 'she' in turn and 'parent' for the person caring for the child.

Parent power

If you feel you're going round in circles, don't forget how much you've already taught your children. **You** are the expert and **you** know what is likely to work with your child. There are no magic answers but change is possible and you can make it happen.

Looking after you

When you are tired and stressed it is hard to be calm and patient. If you feel good about yourself you will find it easier to cope with difficult situations.

So:

- Make time for you.
- Give yourself the occasional treat.
- Praise yourself when you've managed a difficult situation.

Parents need allies

It is important to have an ally on this journey because:

- Talking through a problem helps to work out what is going on.
- It helps you stay calm when your child's behaviour is challenging.
- You need encouragement to stick with a new approach.

Choose a partner, parent or friend who will support you, help you explore ideas for change and back you up.

Children know which parent is a 'soft touch' and learn to ask whoever is most likely to say yes! It is a good idea to agree on the important points with your partner but accept that your styles of parenting may be different. Then settle disagreements as pleasantly as possible. That way you give your children a good model of how to negotiate and compromise.

Children know which parent is a 'soft touch'...

Where behaviour comes from

All behaviour is driven by the child's need and therefore serves a purpose. Understanding what that need is gives you a key to the behaviour. It may be simple or complex, but often a small change can make a big difference.

A child who has high self-esteem and feels good about herself is likely to be at peace with the world and eager to co-operate. Generally children want to please and to behave well, so new, irritating or unco-operative behaviour may be:

- Copied from others.
- Testing boundaries.
- A plea for more attention.
- A reaction to frustration.

It is easy to miss the trigger for challenging behaviour and your reaction may keep feeding the problem. So spend a little time thinking about what could be behind the behaviour.

Reasons for changes in behaviour

Is it a simple reason?

- Hunger.
- Tiredness.
- Boredom or frustration.

Is it a more complex reason?

- Anger or resentment.
- Anxiousness or unhappiness.
- Does she want, or need, more attention?
- Are you expecting too much?
- Does he think you'll give in?
- Does she want to be in control?
- Does he need to prove himself?

Has there been a recent change that could have caused powerful feelings?

- In the family with a birth or death?
- At school with a new year, new teacher, friends?
- Has the child been ill?

Once you have an idea about what your child is feeling you can then respond to their need and be in a better position to help them change their behaviour.

If you think it may be because of:

- **Hunger** - have a snack ready when they come out of school.
- **Tiredness** - make bedtime a little earlier or cut down on after school activities.
- **Boredom** - introduce a new activity such as football club or Brownies.
- **Recent changes** - talk about the change and encourage him to explain how he feels. This will help him cope with his feelings.

Strategies to get the behaviour you want

Think about the behaviour you want and build the following ideas into your whole way of managing your children and, if they are used consistently, they will encourage cooperation.

Check the basics

Build your child's self-esteem

- Tell them often that you love them, even when you don't like their behaviour.
- Praise them for the little things they get right, especially after you have been cross (because they did something wrong).
- Give each child some individual attention every day, play a game of their choice, do some cooking or wash the car together.
- Let them know you enjoy their company.
- Make him feel confident he can behave better by reacting to unacceptable behaviour with a response like: *'That's not like you. You are usually a very kind boy'.*

Keep things positive

- Give little surprises; make a face on their pizza; leave a note by their bed appreciating something about them, *'I love your friendly smile'*.
- Keep a list of fun activities for use when the going gets tough; build a campfire in the garden; have a Smartie hunt; make a camp under the table with a blanket and cushions.
- Talk through the *'story of the day'* at bedtime to celebrate successes and to reinforce expectations if there has been any 'bad' behaviour during the day. Always end on a positive note with a fresh start the next day.

Reduce problems

- **Explain your reasons for rules and requests.**
- **Tell your child what you want, not what you don't.** We tend to draw attention to the behaviour we don't want rather than telling them what we do expect. So say, *'Please keep your feet on the floor'* rather than *'Don't kick the chair'*.
- **Ask only genuine questions**. We often ask a question when we are really giving an instruction. This can frustrate a child if we don't respect their response. So unless you are prepared to get the answer *'no'*, be definite about what you want and say, *'Please take your shoes off before you come in'* or *'It's time to come in for tea now'* rather than *'Would you take your shoes off before you come inside please?'* or *'Shall we have tea now?'*
- **Acknowledge their efforts**. Notice when they do what you ask quickly, are helpful or kind. Not only will they be more likely to do it again but you'll make them feel good about themselves and boost their self-esteem. Give them a smile, a thumbs-up or words of encouragement like *'Well done for doing your coat up / taking your clothes to your room'*, or, *'Thank you for putting your plate in the sink / shutting the door'*.

Giving choices

We all like to feel we are in control of our own lives and can get irritated or angry if we feel we are being *'bossed about'*. Children feel much the same, so look for times when they can learn to take responsibility.

Being responsible means weighing up the pros and cons of an action and making a choice. This involves stopping and thinking, skills all children need if they are to manage their emotions, their friendships and their lives well. To help your child learn these skills offer age-appropriate choices.

- Give a choice between two things from an early age.
- Increase the complexity of choices as children get older.

For example:
'You can have a bath before tea or after tea. It's your choice.'
'Shall I turn off the TV or will you? It's your choice.'
'Would you like to wear your navy trousers or your green ones?'

Giving attention

- Respond to requests for attention.
- Give attention for good behaviour rather than bad.
- Help children to learn to wait.

Attention is like hunger, children vary in the amount they need depending on what stage they are at and upon the circumstances. The arrival of a new baby, a house move or parents separating can all unsettle a child. Then they may need more attention and reassurance than usual.

A child may demand more attention at times.

A child needing attention will literally *'do anything'* to get it, even if that means being shouted at or being told off. If she is clearly showing that she needs more attention, don't be afraid to give it. It is more effective to give positive attention when you choose to than to give negative attention when you are forced to do so by 'bad' behaviour.

Children need to learn to wait for attention, but teach them in small steps. Avoid difficulties by recognising how long your child can wait and respond within that time frame. Then experience teaches them that their needs will be met.

Even brief moments of extra attention can make a difference. Try to increase your interactions with him by smiling at him more frequently, talking to her in the car, involving him in preparing food, getting her to help to pair up the socks.

If you are on the phone, a brief interruption to the call is less disruptive than ignoring him. It will help him to wait if you touch him, give him thumbs-up or make eye contact. Let him know you know he is waiting, then he won't get frustrated and start behaving in a way that will force you to pay attention to him.

Being assertive

Being an assertive parent means being loving, fair, positive, consistent and setting boundaries.

We only need to act assertively when there is something that has to be done and we need our children to comply. Children know when you mean what you say. They see it in your face, hear it in your clear, calm, firm tone and in the direct way you speak.

Acting assertively means:
Saying what you mean,
Meaning what you say,
Sticking with it and
Following through.
(Lee Canter, Assertive Discipline for Parents 1988)

Put these words up as a reminder for when your patience is being tried.

It can help to get down to their level...

Say what you mean and mean what you say

- Take a moment to decide what you will say and how you will say it. Check that you mean it and can follow through.
- Move close to him and speak assertively so that he knows you mean what you say. With a young child it can help to get down to their level, put your hands gently on his shoulders or hold his hands while you speak to him.
- Use her name firmly and calmly.
- Wait for him to respond to be sure you have his attention. Make eye contact.
- Take control by saying, *'I want you to …'* or *'It's time to …'*. For example, *'It's time to turn off the telly now and go up to bed'*.

Stick with it

If your child doesn't do as you ask, or gives an excuse for not complying, or attempts to bargain, do not to be drawn into discussion or argument.

- Repeat your statement in the same firm, calm tone and think what reasonable and realistic sanction you will use if the child chooses not to do it.

If this second request gets no response:

- Repeat the instruction and tell him the sanction that will follow if he makes a bad choice: *'Take turns with the bike or it will go in the shed. It's your choice.'* Or,
'You can come in for tea now or stay out and lose time for TV later. It's your choice.' Or,
'Turn off the telly and go up to bed now or tomorrow bedtime will be half an hour earlier.'

Using the words *'it's your choice'* tells the child clearly that what happens is up to her and not some nasty punishment by a cruel parent.

Follow through

Then make sure that bedtime **is** earlier the next night!

When you first use this approach you will find that your child may be angrier than ever, because she thinks you will give in if she carries on long enough. Stick with it, even if you get a tantrum, and you will find she learns that you mean what you say.

Don't remind him of the behaviour you didn't want, *'You didn't do as you were told'*, or add insult to injury by adding, *'it's your own fault'*.

Instead be sympathetic with her frustration and remind her of what she can do the next time; that way you help her take responsibility for her behaviour: *'I know you are cross you made a bad choice, but if you stay in bed tonight you can earn extra time for tomorrow'*.

Setting boundaries

We all need some structure in our lives since we function better if we know roughly what the day holds. Family life runs more smoothly when everybody automatically carries out the daily routine, when everyone knows the limits and when expectations are clear.

Children feel safe and secure with a framework of rules and routines so that they know where they are and what is expected of them.

Family rules

- Make rules age appropriate.
- Agree rules with your child.
- Explain why they are important.

Parents need to agree the rules between them, and then explain them, and the reason for having them, to their children.

Family rules need to be appropriate for the age of the child and they need to be reviewed as children grow older. Young children generally respect age-appropriate rules: *'The rule is you always hold hands to cross the road'*.

Children also learn that rules in one family are not necessarily the same as in other families but that some rules are absolutes such as: *'We don't take things that don't belong to us'*.

Routines

- Use routines from a young age.
- Keep routines flexible.
- Involve your child in developing and adapting routines.

As a family, decide on the way you want to do things. Then do everyday activities in the same way. You'll find that you've already established quite a few helpful routines that:

- Reduce arguments.
- Establish good habits.
- Set a framework for each new day that makes life run more smoothly.
- Help busy parents manage complex lifestyles with less friction and anxiety.

Children feel more secure if they have routines they are familiar with. Review your routines from time to time.

From quite a young age children can help to plan how you do things. This develops a sense of responsibility and increases their self-confidence and self-esteem as they realise that they are important members of the family team.

Every family is different but some key routines are:

- **Getting out in the morning.** Put on the clothes that have been put out the night before, go downstairs, have breakfast, clean teeth and then play until it's time to put on shoes and coat and go to school.
- **Who's looking after them?** Who will fetch them from nursery; are they going straight home after school or to the childminder?
- **Homework or reading practice.** This fits into life more smoothly if it is always done at a regular time - straight after tea or as soon as they get home.
- **Helping at home.** As children get older having a rota for helping with the dishes, or feeding the cat, develops a sense of responsibility and helps stop arguments about turns.

Routines can always be put on one side because of some unexpected event or for a special treat, *'because it's a lovely day and we want to go to the park'.*

Negotiating

- Involve your child in planning ahead of time.
- Make time to listen to your child's point of view.
- Sympathise with the child's frustration.

All children will occasionally challenge authority but no family can afford the time to negotiate even a fraction of their many daily decisions. That is where rules and routines come to the rescue.

But when you feel your child has a genuine objection you need to decide whether you must stand firm or whether there is room for negotiation. Either way you need to state the reason for your decision, thus remaining in charge while respecting their wishes where possible.

- **Parental decision.** *'You have to get into the car now because we have no food in the house and I need to get something to cook for tea.'*
- **Negotiated decision.** *'OK. I understand you don't want to go shopping now. We have to go sometime this afternoon but we could go later. Can we agree when would be a good time?'*

Negotiation should involve the parents and each child expressing their wishes and the reasons for them. Children can often suggest a range of compromises and, with help, accept one of them as a solution.

Listening is the key to reaching an agreement. Even if the outcome is not to the child's liking he will find it easier to accept if he feels he has been listened to. If they get frustrated, angry or resentful about the decision then sympathise with their feelings.

If you can, negotiate beforehand, then you avoid an argument and what might be seen as a climb down. Try discussing *'the plan for the day'* first thing in the morning as part of the daily routine. Then children know what's happening and can negotiate ahead of time.

Contracts

- Contracts need to be agreed by all parties involved.
- Contracts may be informal or written down.
- Contracts need to include the conditions and sanctions.

Contracts are individual routines negotiated with older children, aged eight or more. Use them as a way of changing or improving behaviour provided both parties agree the terms and conditions.

Contracts are often made on the spur of the moment: *'You may go to play on your bike so long as you are home by 7 o'clock, otherwise it will be no bike tomorrow. OK?'*

For more persistent problems it works best to sit down quietly together and talk about your contract. Try to include:

- **What the agreement is about.** *'Jolene can go to Katie's house every Tuesday after school'.*
- **The conditions that apply.** *'Jolene will do her homework as soon as she gets home.'* And *'Jolene will call home before she leaves Katie's at half past five.'*
- **The rewards and sanctions.** *'If Jolene fails to keep the agreement she will not be allowed to go the following week.'*
- **When the contract will be discussed again.**

If the contract is about a regular event your child might find it helpful to stick a reminder up in a prominent place, particularly if there has been a failure to keep to the agreement.

Trying new strategies

If you always do
what you've always done
you'll always get
what you always got.
(Candida Hunt, The Parenting Puzzle (2006)

If what you are doing isn't working, try something different. Choose your strategy to fit the situation and your child - even small changes can make a big difference.

Distraction

Shift their attention to something else, real or imaginary.

- **In the supermarket.** *'Oh goodness, I've forgotten to get the cereal. What shall we have this week?'*
- **In the car.** *'Look, is that a fire engine down the road?'*
- **At home.** Talk to yourself about some new activity that might move things on, *'I was thinking we might make some biscuits. I wonder, shall we make chocolate or raisin ones?'*

Challenge

Challenge her to see if:

- She can get her shoes on before you count to ten.
- He can stay in his own bed.
- Whether she is old enough to be in charge of putting her own bike away?

Reminders

Remind her of the occasion when she was successful, the night he did stay in his bed or she played well with her brother, and tell him how pleased you were.

Confidence

Say something confidently like, *'I know you can do it'.*

Humour

Share a funny story with another child or suddenly remember a joke. *'Have you heard the one about ....?'*

Games

Make a game of it: *'Let's take turns to put the toys in the box'.* Or say to the child in a strop, *'Let's both stamp our feet'.*

Warnings

Giving children 5 minutes warning will help them prepare to do something they aren't keen on, or to stop doing something they're enjoying.

- Say, *'In 2 / 5 / 10 minutes (depending on the age of the child) it will be time for tea or bed or homework'.*
- Set a timer, then the bell is the signal rather than you *'nagging'* or *'going on'.*

Clarity

Tell them exactly what you want: *'I'd like to see those toys back in the box'* or, *'We agreed you would do your homework before tea'.*

Trickery

The next time a small child who is always saying *'no'* says *'no',* immediately ask them a question that requires a 'yes' answer:

'Is your name Brooklyn / Sarah / Imran?'
'Are you three / four / five?'

Continue asking questions that require a *'yes'* answer and then pop in the original question that got the *'no'* answer. It can work in a light-hearted way to break the habit of saying *'no'* and change resistance into cooperation.

Surprise

This strategy is perhaps best kept for home use. Diffuse the confrontation by making them laugh with the *'tickle treatment'*. You have to judge the moment and the child. If you get it wrong you could have a major tantrum on your hands.

You'll have to judge if the moment is right for the tickle treatment.

Acknowledging behaviour

Rewards

We all like to have our helpful or 'good' behaviour noticed. We appreciate it when someone says 'thank you' or gives us flowers or chocolates, when we have made an effort. It makes us feel good about ourselves and we are more likely to repeat our helpful behaviour. So don't worry that giving rewards and incentives to children for behaviour they *'ought'* to do is bribery.

Adults can promise themselves a cup of tea or time looking at the telly for finishing an unpleasant job. This privilege is not available to children, so you need to:

- Acknowledge positive behaviour.
- Be clear what it is you are pleased with.
- Use extra rewards carefully.

Praise and appreciation

Praise that is honest and heartfelt and lets the child know **what** you are pleased about is a powerful tool - use it carefully!
'I like the way you shared your toy with Molly.'
'It makes me happy when you come as soon as I call you'.
To encourage the behaviour you want and increase your child's self-esteem show your appreciation with a:

- Smile
- Hug
- Pat on the back
- Thumbs up
- Hand clap.

Treats and privileges

If your child doesn't respond to praise then consider some of the following:

- More of your time, perhaps reading a story with you.
- Something to do, like going to the park.
- Something to eat or choosing what's for tea.
- Something to have, such as a new pencil or a small toy.
- A treat, like ten minutes extra TV.

Rewards charts

You can inspire your child to aim high and reach a target.

For young children draw a picture for them to colour in a section each time they are successful. Children aren't fussy about the quality of the drawing so let them choose an image and get drawing. Or use your imagination and make a ladder with a figure to move up it, or a rocket to reach the moon - using Blu-Tack to hold them in place.

Charts on which the child can record her own progress can work well with the over threes and are particularly useful with older children. You can use a simple star chart like this:

Alex's getting himself dressed chart

Monday	Tuesday	Wednesday	Thursday	Friday	Saturday	Sunday
*	*		*		*	*
*	*	*		*	*	*

Keep things positive and never put crosses in the boxes when success is not achieved. You could give an extra reward when there is a star in, say, three consecutive boxes.

Timing of Rewards

As a rough guide a three-year-old needs to receive a 'long term' reward within the day, a six-year-old can keep up their enthusiasm for three or four days, an eight-year-old can manage up to a week before receiving their reward.

So make sure you draw a realistic number of sections to colour, or rungs to climb, or stars to collect.

Family Treats

These can work well as brothers and sisters then have an interest in encouraging the target child to behave better. It is important to make it clear to the family when the treat will happen and to think of something that will work for your particular child.

Don't get carried away in your desperation for a full night's sleep or for siblings to stop fighting. Beware promising *'any toy you want'* or *'a bicycle'*. It could be an expensive week!

Sometimes brothers and sisters can demand rewards too. So set them a target for something they find difficult to do. That way you can work on the whole family's behaviour!

Don't get carried away with rewards - it could be expensive!

Rewarding older children

Older children respond very differently to rewards. They still want your love and approval but are wary of the big public demonstrations that toddlers thrive on. A quiet word of appreciation, a text message, being excused the chores, a lift to their friend's house, or money can be more powerful incentives for older children.

Punishment or consequence?

A **punishment** is imposed by someone bigger and stronger. It may stop the behaviour in the short term but can create feelings of anger, resentment and revenge. Punishment does not help children understand how they should have behaved.

A **consequence**, or sanction, should make sense to your child and follow logically from what she has done.

- If they throw their drink on the floor they must clean up the mess.
- If they deliberately break someone else's toy they lose their pocket money to help pay for a new toy.
- If they leave their bike out on the street it remains in the shed for a day.

To be effective a consequence should:

- be as small as possible
- be something the child dislikes
- not be physically or psychologically damaging
- be followed by a fresh start.

Give him a chance to behave appropriately as soon as possible. Sending him to his room for an hour means he'll find something to do and forget why he was sent there.

It is no good taking away TV time if the child prefers to play with his cars. Children will sometimes pretend not to care about a sanction. Don't be fooled, it is usually bluff! You need to calmly continue to impose the sanction you said would follow.

Once a child has suffered the consequence of their bad behaviour it is important to start afresh without blame and without seeking promises of future good behaviour. Assume she is going to behave well; expectations are very powerful.

Responding to 'bad' behaviour

- **Keep calm and use a quiet voice**. Cool things down by asking a rude or demanding child to repeat her request politely and in a quiet voice.
- **Say 'yes' not 'no'.** Prevent an argument by giving a conditional *'yes'* rather than a *'no but'*, *'Yes, when you have done your homework'* or *'Yes, tomorrow'*. A *'yes'* puts him in a more cooperative frame of mind.
- Listen to her explanation for her behaviour.
- Be cross with the deed not the child. *'Knocking over your drink has made a terrible mess. I am cross about that'* not *'You are a naughty boy'*.
- Avoid labelling. If you give children labels they tend to live up to them so don't say, *'You are a very naughty girl'* or *'You are a liar'*.
- Think carefully before saying *'never'* and *'always'*. Give the child the belief that he can do the right thing by being positive. Say: 'You are usually so good at doing what I ask', rather than, *'You never do as you are told'* and, *'You usually like your peas'* rather than *'You always leave your dinner'*.

Attention-seeking behaviour

- Act quickly and calmly.
- Remove the child or yourself from the scene.
- Don't be drawn into arguments.

We often give our most animated response to the behaviour we don't want. We move in close, raise our voice and spend longer talking to them than when they are 'good'.

So if you think your child's behaviour is designed to get your attention, it is best to pay as little notice to the 'bad' behaviour as possible. Prompt him about what he should be doing and make it clear that you will only respond when he asks in a quiet voice. If you have said *'no'* stick with it. Try using distraction or warn him of the consequences if he chooses to continue.

If that doesn't work then ignoring is often the best option. Try turning your back or going into another room. Be sure to give positive attention as soon as he behaves appropriately.

Ignoring is often the best option.

Behaviour you can't ignore

When behaviour is dangerous or destructive, you need to intervene quickly, but avoid eye contact and sermonising.

When children's emotions are aroused they are not able to hear and take in reasons. Say, *'No, I know you are angry but you may not kick / throw something / hurt me'*, firmly and calmly without looking at her. This is more effective than listing all the reasons. Have a quiet talk later when she's calmed down and is able to listen to you.

Time Out

Giving children *Time Out* gives them the chance to calm down and think about what they've done.

Make a small chair, or the bottom of the stairs, the Thinking Chair or Step. This emphasises the need for them to think about their behaviour and what they should have done instead.

Only leave a child in Time Out for one minute for each year of his age, or he'll quickly forget why he is there and find something to do to entertain himself. It is unwise to use the cot or bedroom as the *Time Out* place - you don't want it to be associated with punishment.

Planning for change

When you are ready to make a change, then plan your approach with your partner or a friend. Choose a child-free time, when you have a reasonable amount of energy and the family situation is calm - not just before you go on holiday, when granddad is coming to stay or you've just come home from hospital.

First steps

To help you make sense of what is going on, write down your answers to these questions:

- What's the child doing?
- What's behind it?
  - Can I meet the need some other way?
- When does it happen?
  - Can I change the routine?
- Where does it happen?
  - Can I avoid going there with the child?
- Who does it happen with?
  - Can someone else take over?
- Is what I am expecting of my child reasonable?
- Do I talk to the child enough about the behaviour I want?
- Can I give the child more warning?
- Do I give the child enough praise for good behaviour?
- What rewards can I use?
- What consequences will I use?
- Have I got a plan?

You may find some strategies immediately spring to mind, especially if you look back through this booklet. Now write out a six point plan following the steps below.

Your six point plan

1. My child needs to do...
2. The reward for success will be...
3. To be sure rewards are given and sanctions kept to, our record will be...
4. To be sure of success I will change what I do by...
5. If the child is successful I will react by...
6. If the child is NOT successful I will react by...

Here are some examples:

A six point plan for Tom (aged 3-4) who keeps coming downstairs after being put to bed.

1.	Tom needs to...	... stay in bed once we've said good night.
2.	The reward for success will be...	... We'll be very pleased and he can stay up 5 mins later the next night.
3.	Our record will be...	... We'll make sure we both know whether or not he earned an extra 5 mins stay up time.
4.	We will change what we do by...	... Dad will make sure that Tom has plenty of exercise during the day. We'll make Tom's bedtime a little later and spend a short time (5-10 mins) with him in bed, reading or talking so he is settled and ready to sleep. Obvious excuses for getting up will have been dealt with e.g. toilet and drink. After we say 'Goodnight' we'll respond to further requests only with, 'It's time to settle down' or 'In the morning'.
5.	If Tom is successful I/we will react by...	... We'll make a big song and dance about it in the morning, praising him for his 'good choice' (including any siblings that have also stayed in bed) and remind him of his extra staying up time.
6.	If Tom is not successful I/we will react by...	... We will return him to bed quickly and firmly without comment. If he chooses to get up he will not earn an extra 5 mins 'stay up late' next day.

A six point plan for Rupa (aged 7) who leaves her bike on the street

1.	Rupa needs to...	... put her bike in the hallway when she is called in for tea.
2.	The reward for success will be...	... We'll praise her for looking after her bike.
3.	Our record will be...	... No record needed because Dad or Mum will immediately lock the bike.
4.	We will change what we do by...	... We'll remind her when she goes out about bringing in her bike.
5.	If Rupa is successful I/we will react by...	... We'll praise her immediately for looking after her bike and remind her of one of the good reasons for bringing it in: • it won't get stolen or borrowed • it won't get rusty in the rain • she'll know where it is when she wants to go out.
6.	If Rupa is not successful I/we will react by...	... We will not nag, criticise or comment but will calmly send her straight back out to get her bike. It will be padlocked and doesn't go out the following day.

See the plan through

Make sure that all the adults involved with the family understand the plan and that they agree to follow it when dealing with the child's behaviour.

Find a quiet time to talk to your child about the plan. Explain what you want her to do and why. With an older child, if there is room for compromise, it may be appropriate to negotiate a contract between you.

- Tell him what is in it for him – both the rewards and the sanctions.
- Tell her you know she can do it and point out how much happier you and she will feel when the problem is sorted.
- Tell him when the plan will start.
- Be positive and predict success.

Once you put your plan into practice try to be consistent. You may find that at first your child tests you to see if you really mean it. You may not see immediate improvements but persist, you should see some changes within two weeks.

If you can keep a written record of your progress it will help in the next stage. It might look something like this:

Jo's staying in bed record: each tick records a time that Jo gets out of bed and calls us or comes downstairs. SUCCESS will be when there have been no ticks for three consecutive days.						
Monday	Tuesday	Wednesday	Thursday	Friday	Saturday	Sunday
✓✓✓✓✓✓	✓✓✓✓✓✓	✓✓	*	✓✓✓✓	✓✓	
	✓✓✓	✓	✓✓✓✓		✓	
	SUCCESS					

Review and change

After three weeks you need to review your plan and decide whether you need to make any changes. If you have been successful you can celebrate and start to ease off the plan. Go back to it if your child has a relapse.

If you have not yet been successful have a careful look at your plan and ask yourself the following:

- Are you expecting too much?
- Do you need to change the reward because your child isn't interested or it's not powerful enough?
- Do you need to go back to the beginning and think about the child's 'need'? Is Jo not tired enough, frightened of the picture on the wall, disturbed by the noise of the TV?
- Is there something you can change so that you can adjust your plan and try again?

Other sources of help

If you feel you are still stuck then it is time to seek outside help. Have a word with:

- Your child's nursery or school.
- Your Health Visitor / clinic.
- From a telephone helpline or website (your local Council will have a Children's Information Service).
- Your GP.

Some helpful websites include:

www.parentlineplus.org
www.parentinguk.org
www.singleparents.org.uk
www.parentscentre.gov.uk/ Parents Centre is a site that contains advice for parents, helping you to help your child.

Telephone numbers:

Details of your local Children's Information service in England are available from ChildcareLink freephone 0800 2 346346
Twin line 0800 138 0509

Books to read:

The Parenting Puzzle by Candida Hunt,
ISBN 978-0954470906, published by Family Links.
Toddler Taming by Christopher Green,
ISBN 978-0091902582, published by Vermilion.
Beyond Toddlerdom by Christopher Green,
ISBN 978-0091816247, published by Vermilion.